MOBILE MONEY MACHINE

(How to use your Smartphone to make REAL MONEY NOW)

BY

THOMAS H. JOHNSON, MBA, CPA

MOBILE MONEY MACHINE

Copyright © 2015 Thomas H. Johnson

ISBN-13: 978-1517057916

First Edition

DISCLAIMER: This book is about sharing ideas, tips, tricks and suggestions on ways to reduce your costs and help make you extra money. I am in no way giving any kind of financial or legal advice and take no responsibility for any liability or loss they may result from you using the advice in this book. You need to make sure you read the terms and use of any website or application that you download and/or use and any restrictions that may exist with its use.

INTRODUCTION

I want to say thank you for purchasing my book "Mobile Money Machine". I really do appreciate you spending your hard earned money on this book, and more importantly, your valuable time. I promise to make very good use of your time and truly hope you find significant value in what you learn. I firmly believe that if you use only one or two of the many ideas presented in this book, you will easily recoup your investment.

In today's highly mobile world it is essential that you have the tools and techniques to maximize every transaction that you make. I will share with you dozens of ideas on how to reduce your costs or increase your cash by leveraging the most powerful device you own, your Smartphone. Many of the ideas are simple and can be implemented immediately, whereas other ideas will take a little more effort to make them happen. I assure you that the extra efforts are more than worth your time.

Throughout this book you will encounter three central concepts that are critical to making the most of the strategies that I have outlined in this book. These ideas work in the mobile world for sure, however, they also work with any type of purchase once you have mastered them. I encourage you to take the time to truly study these concepts and think about how you can apply them on your next financial transaction, buying or selling.

The first strategy I want you to learn is the ideal of **STACKING** your purchases. Stacking means that anytime you make a purchase, either in-store or online, you will be trying to "stack up" your discounts. A 20% coupon code, a price match from a competitor, a product write down, buy one get one, cash back, free shipping, etc.

The second strategy is called **BUNDLING** your purchases. Bundling explores the idea of looking for opportunities to add extra items that lowers your overall total net cost of your bundled purchase. So if you buy something online for $45 and free shipping starts for orders at $50, add an item for $5. Or if you buy an appliance, bundle in free delivery and setup, free removal and disposal of your old one, extra warranty on your new unit, any consumables that you may need. If you are buying a car, ask for mats and flaps, free inspections and/or oil changes for life.

The last strategy is called **NESTING** or **LINKING** your online activities to create self-sustaining investments. The idea here is that your transactions will create a stream of cash that can be invested by linking your accounts to tax advantaged programs. These programs generate more cash, which can be reinvested into the system, and on and on, thereby making it self-sustaining. This concept takes a little more effort to understand and implement, however, I will outline it for you to make it easier to accomplish.

I have broken this book out into two major sections: Section 1 focuses on the buying side of your transactions by reducing your total dollars spent using mobile apps and the three strategies that I just described. Section 2 focuses more on the selling side of your transactions, where you are using mobile apps to make money from your activities which also leverages the three strategies.

I want to encourage you to not become overwhelmed with all these ideas and strategies. Try them one at a time and incrementally build upon them. Have fun with them, and make a game out of it. See how much you can save or make using your new found mobile apps. See how many things you can stack, bundle or link together to create a new value that didn't exist before. Be creative and use your imagination to create something new, no matter how small. Lastly, track your progress so you can see the results of your efforts and take credit for your successes. You deserve it! OK, here we go, buckle up!

SECTION 1 – Buy Side Transactions

UPROMISE

I am a big fan of Upromise (www.upromise.com) and I highly recommend using their click through service to capture affiliate generated cash back. Basically, how this works is that Upromise signs up as an affiliate with hundreds of companies that are willing to pay them an affiliate commission i.e., a percentage of the sale, to drive traffic to their website.

Once you become a member of Upromise, you go to the Upromise site and search for the products and companies you want to buy from and "click through" to their site. This process passes the affiliate member ID to the company you are buying from so they know to pay Upromise, and you the member, the sales commission.

Commissions can range from a paltry 1%, up to a hefty 25% for each qualifying purchase. There are some companies that pay a flat dollar amount such as $25 or $75 per purchase event, like a new cell phone activation. There are also coupon codes for discounts and free shipping, etc. Think about how many times you have shopped online and missed out on these commissions? They can amount to thousands of dollars per year depending on how much you spend.

Some members that have been in the program for many years have reported earning over $10,000 in cash back so far, not to mention the thousands of dollars in discounts on the retail purchase price. You can direct these funds into your kids college funds (qualifying and linked IRS 529 Plans) or to a high yield saving account (with a 10% annual bonus with Sallie Mae) or even request a check be sent directly to you.

To get the most out of the program you really need to sign up for the Upromise branded MasterCard which is currently offered through Barclays Bank. Once you get your credit card you need to register it, and any other credit cards you have, including grocery loyalty cards, on the Upromise website so they can track your purchases and ensure you get credit for your transactions. The card also pays you 1% cash back on all purchases.

NESTING EFFECT

The nesting effect (feedback loop) is a self sustaining process that grows and expands as a direct result of using the Upromise program if setup correctly. What I mean by this is that you can setup your account to automatically transfer your cash back into a tax deductible college 529-plan, or High Yield savings account. Each month you will earn interests, dividends or capital gains (depending on your investments) all from free money that will then generate additional free money. If you reinvest all the gains the compounding effects can be huge.

Once you file your tax return, you will most likely get a refund from your state (check with your state) for all those contributions made to your 529 plan. Take that refund and put it back into your 529 plan, this combined with the continued contributions from your Upromise account, will continue to grow your account with zero dollars out of your pocket.

The same logic holds true for the high yield savings account (www.salliemae.com) which will pay you a 10% bonus, calculated from the total Upromise contributions for the year, paid in February in the following year. This again is free money on top of free money that will continue to generate additional gains for you as long as you keep shopping through Upromise, using the credit card and grocery loyalty cards.

The Upromise program is flexible so that you can contribute to both a 529 plan and a high yielding saving account. You can specify the percentage of dollars sent to each linked account however you would like. I use them both and sometimes change the percentages depending upon my short and long term investment goals.

Here is another good strategy to consider, sometimes I buy restaurant/store gift certificates through Upromise and get the cash back (some do not allow this). Then once I get the gift cards I go online and buy the products that I wanted, through Upromise of course, and get additional cash back. Many times there are also coupons codes offered through Upromise. Don't forget to check with some of the other coupon sites like www.retailmenot.com or www.couponcabin.com or www.groupon.com that allow you to STACK your discounts.

Also, if you have and use the Upromise branded credit card, which I highly recommend, to make your purchases, they kick you back another 5% or more. I have been able to achieve greater than 50% off my purchase once I am finished with all my discount coupon codes, affiliate cash back and credit card rebates. I make it a game to see how much I can trim of the retail price of a product.

Upromise recently launched a mobile app that allows you to do a quick search of participating companies based on your location or zip code. This is helpful when you are traveling and looking for ways to save and get cash back for gas, food and in-store retailers. They also have a program called RewardU that you can load on your connected devices that automatically keeps track of the sites you visit so that you do not miss getting credit for your purchases. Very nice!

Upromise is an amazing program with many different ways for you to earn cash back from your shopping activities. I just covered a few of the key elements of the program. However, you can earn cash from doing web searches, using credit cards, dining, gas, and coupons for groceries, discounts on products, travel, friends and families shopping, in-store retail, and on and on. They keep expanding their services and offering new ways to earn for things you do all the time. You are doing these activities anyway; you may as well get paid for it!

If you find that the company you want to buy from is not a participating Upromise affiliate, there are other companies that offer similar click through commissions. Check out www.topcashback.com and www.ebates.com to see if they are listed there. I would recommend joining them as well so that you rarely miss out on a purchase commission.

Google search "affiliate commissions" or other keywords to see what other companies are out there. It seems like more and more are getting into the game. The same goes for "coupon codes" and other discounting and linking opportunities. Every time I do more research on this topic, more and more new startup companies are finding new approaches to offering savvy shoppers the opportunity to save and/or get cash back from their activities.

WALMART SAVING CATCHER

When Walmart launched their new app called "Saving Catcher", I downloaded it immediately and began reaping the benefits. How this app works is that each time you make a purchase at Walmart you scan your receipt using the app. It then searches all the competing stores in your area for the same items. If the app finds a lower price at another store, it gives you the difference back on a Walmart e-gift card that you can use for a future purchase.

I have only had this app for a few months but the savings are accruing very quickly. Sometimes I am saving 5% to 10% for a shopping trip. I prefer to save up my credits until they reach $25, which I then convert to an e-gift card for my next visit.

I also found that you can scan in up to 7 receipts per week. Sometime I have to go to the store many times per week since I often forget items or have an unexpected need or birthday present that I need to buy.

It is amazing to me how something so simple that requires so little effort can produce so much value. I am guessing that I will have over $500 in saving in about a year's time. Not bad for doing something that I would probably be doing every week anyhow, like shopping at Walmart.

GAS BUDDY

Here is another essential, no-brainer must have app. I use this app at least every other week when it comes time to fill the tank on the car. It literally takes me ten seconds to pull up the app, scan my area by zip code and BOOM up comes a list of all the gas stations in the area sorted by lowest price. There is usually a $.10 to $.15 difference between the lowest price and the area average, which calculates into $2.20 to $3.30 saving for me (I have a 22 gallon gas tank). Annualize this at 30 fill ups per year and you have $66 to $99 savings. Not bad for a completely free app and very little time investment.

But wait! There's MORE! If it happens to be at a gas station where I have a loyalty card, like Sheetz, then I get an additional $.03 per gallon, or an additional $.66. If it is an Exxon station, Upromise participating company, I can get $.01 per gallon cash back and an additional 3% of the total purchase, plus another 1% cash back when I use my Upromise credit card. It is becoming difficult to keep up with all the STACKED savings when buying gas for the car.

Some people are big on buying their groceries at some of the major chains that offer gas rewards as a perk for shopping there and using their customer loyalty cards. I often hear boasting at the office, "I just got $2.00 off per gallon" or "I got a free fill up" because I get my groceries at this place or that place. Think about it folks, you are overpaying for the groceries to offset the cost of the gas discounts. I know this to be true because I have checked a lot of prices between the large grocery chains and I am an avid user of the Walmart saving catcher app.

This app shows you very clearly which stores beat Walmart's pricing and by how much. There is a clear pattern of overpricing by certain chains that offer the big gas rewards. I skip the gas rewards and go directly to the discounted items from the get go. There are always those "loss leader" items that every chain uses to get people in the door in hopes that they will buy some of the other overpriced items. I know some people that will load up on gift cards for other stores and restaurants to get loads of gas points from the grocery retailer.

This is an OK idea however; I think it will probably lead to overspending by over buying gift cards that you may not really need.

AMAZON

It's really difficult to not be a fan of Amazon "the online marketplace to the world of everything". I am Prime member and buy almost all of my entertainment from them, which is all stored in their cloud forever. Think about it, I buy a movie from them using their video streaming service and now I own it. It doesn't get scratched, lost, stolen or borrowed.

I have hundreds of songs, movies, apps and games hosted by Amazon for me in their cloud for free. You can regularly find opportunities to get free Amazon e-gift cards for attending webinars and online surveys. They can add up quickly so that many of the movies you buy are free. Also, if you have kids, they will get to enjoy all this content for free as well as generation to come.

I love to use Amazon price checker app anytime I am looking to buy something in-store. They are my benchmark and "gold standard" to compare all others. When I go into a store looking for something, I pull out my phone and check the price by scanning the barcode on it to see if the price is competitive. If it's not, I can order it from Amazon right from my phone or take a picture and wait until I get home to shop for a better price.

This only happens after taking into consideration all the other options for discounting and cash back. As you probably have guessed by now, getting the best price can be a lot of work. There are so many options and stacking considerations to account for. Sometimes I don't have the time or the energy so I check Upromise quickly and if they can't get me cash back I just order on Amazon. With the free shipping as a prime member, I have the items in two days and any returns are easy to complete.

One caveat you need to be aware of when shopping online is the emerging concept of "dynamic pricing". I have not been able to pinpoint this with any one company but I have been reading more about it lately. Dynamic pricing is the process in which a company will use advanced analytics to identify and study the buying habits of each online consumer. Based on results of the analytics, they will arrive at the highest price they believe you are likely to pay for an item.

If they see that you quickly look up and item, put into your cart, and then check out right away. They may conclude that you are impulsive and willing to pay a higher price. If you look up the same item over and over for weeks, tracking the price, then you are probably more cost conscious and more likely to only pay less. If they examine your purchase history and you buy a lot of high ticket items, they can infer you are wealthy and will probably charge you more.

I know this doesn't seem fair, and again I haven't caught anyone doing this yet. I just want you to understand that it is possible and that you may what to check prices using private mode in your browser (InPrivate or Incognito). Try using different devices and different browsers to see if you are getting different prices for the same items. My other favorite trick is to put something in an online shopping cart and then not complete the purchase. I just let it sit there for a few days and I wait for an e-mail to come in from the company.

They absolutely hate having stuff sit in the cart that is not purchased. This lowers their conversion rate which is bad for business so they may send you an online coupon or discount code to try to push you to complete that last step. I like to use this time to search for better deals online and in the stores. Sometimes I use the code if they send it and other times I find a better deal elsewhere and empty the cart.

EBAY

I have saved more money by buying on EBay than probably any other site on the Internet. Most people think that it's all just used stuff and that you have to wait 7 days or more for an auction to be completed to see if you were lucky enough to win the bidding war. This is not the case, there are tons of brand new items that are available and can be purchased using the "buy now" features which many of the sellers offer. There are also a lot of companies selling items and online EBay storefronts.

There are lots of tips and tricks to buying on EBay, entire books are written on the subject. If you need an item, check the price here as well. Yes, you can also save a ton if you have the time and patience to participate in the auctions.

CRAIGSLIST

This website is a good local catch all for everything else that may not fit well into the other sites that we have already discussed. So maybe you want to buy a large item like a gun safe or a baby stroller. Not the most ideal type of items for shipping long distances. If you can find them locally on Craigslist and at an awesome price, then go for it. There are some caveats that you need to be aware of with this site though. It is not as "regulated" as the others.

You have be very cautious as to who you are dealing with and protect your privacy as much as you can. If you do agree to a deal with someone, set a meeting place at a local mall or other highly public place to make sure the transaction goes smoothly. I would not get into a habit of telling strangers on the Internet where you live or even work for that matter. Like all business dealings you have to be smart about how you handle things.

I am not singling out Craigslist on this topic; they have a good business that provides a valuable service. I think you need to always be on your guard when doing any business online or in-stores to protect your privacy and identity.

TRAVEL

When you are looking to book travel there is no better site to master than Priceline (www.priceline.com). I have spent countless hours using their tools and studying both their website, and overall business model. It is fascinating to me that I can go on a hotel's website and see the room I want listed at $299 per night, and then go on Priceline and book that same room for $89 per night. Of course, it is not that easy if you are not a master of the tool sets. There is also that bothersome issue of supply and demand. Sometimes when I am trying to get to the big city and there are a lot of popular events going on, hotel rooms are hard to come by.

Priceline, or any travel site, is going to have a hard time finding you discounted rooms.

Priceline, and others, thrive off of excess room capacity. If there are no excess rooms, there are no opportunities for discounts. There are two main ways to find great discounts using the Priceline toolsets. First is by using their Express Deals option to make a direct purchase of a room based on the location and star rating. You won't know the exact name of the hotel you will be getting, but with a little research into the possible options you can get a pretty good idea of who the candidates are likely to be.

Express Deal rates are usually better than the standard listing pricing on the hotels website and the other travel related sites. Also, Priceline will regularly send out online coupon codes for additional saving opportunities for Express Deals. You should sign up on their website to make sure these coupons hit your inbox.

Sometimes in a tight supply market, these coupons make the difference and end up being the best deal in town. The other major way to save is by using their "Name your own Price" tool. This is basically a bidding tool, which allows you to name the price that you want to pay and see if there are any hotels that will accept it. This is my favorite way to buy hotel rooms and it represents the best way to get the ABSOLUTE best price.

I have been able to score very nice 4 star hotels rooms for $65 per night, and then get a free upgrade to an executive suite. This was during the slow season in the dead of winter, but I had to be there anyway so why not stay in luxury!

Like everything else, you need to know how to use the bidding tools to get the best price. I always start with the highest star ratings for the area I am going to visit, four or five star. I look around the market to make sure I know what hotels are there and their star rating. I also check each of their websites for best price and current availability. This gives me a good idea of what the market looks like, supply versus demand.

I then check the Priceline site and see what Express Deals are listed at. If the Express Deals are priced lower, then I know I can get a great rate using the bidding tools. If the Express deals are priced high, meaning closer to the Hotels standard rates, then I know demand is up and I will have a harder time getting an awesome rate.

Travel, like most things, is priced based on the balance between supply and demand. Therefore, you have to have a good sense of the demand for the area you are looking to book before you can set a realistic price target for your booking. I try to set a range of acceptability and go from there. I also look at my past booking history to see what kinds of rates I have paid in the past and during what months to help guide me as well.

The more clues that you can piece together the better the rate you are going to get! Don't forget that Priceline is an Upromise member so add 6% (plus 1% if you use the Upromise credit card) cash back on top of all of the savings you get from using Priceline. Remember, STACK and BUNDLE discounts on every purchase as much as possible to get the total net best price.

As a general guideline, I like to try to get $20 more in savings by using the bidding tool over what is listed as an Express Deal. That is where I start my bidding and I keep raising my offer by $5 increments until I hit the Express deal price or I can use a coupon code to get a lower overall price. This strategy has worked for me almost every time and the savings keep adding up.

There are situations where I need to stay more than one night and I have developed a different strategy for this. Say you want to stay Friday, Saturday and Sunday night in a big city. If you put the three days into the Priceline search tool it will come back and price all three nights at the same price per night.

The rate will be the highest rate for whatever night has the highest demand, say Saturday night. How do I know? Well, check the rates for each night one by one and you will see the large difference in the room rates on a per night basis.

So the logical thing to do is break up your nights and book them all separately, thereby taking advantage of the lowest rate per night for your entire stay. One caveat with this strategy is that you could end up with different hotels and have to check in/out and move to another one for each night. This happened to me last time I was traveling for more than one night.

It may sound a bit inconvenient to have to switch hotels for each night. But I am willing to deal with that to save $230 dollars, which is what my total savings was for the three nights. The other thing with hotels is dealing with the parking when you get there. "Hello sir and welcome to our Hotel, would you like Valet parking for only $30 per day!" My response, heck no!

I can find a mobile app that points me to either free or low cost public parking within a block or two from the hotel. I will park in the check-in stop and stay there while I am checking in and getting ready for wherever I am heading. Take advantage of the free parking for a few hours. Sometimes the valet parks your car since you are taking too long to come down. That's OK that is free as well.

Don't forget to check out the other travel sites as well, like Trivago, Kayak, Expedia, Orbits, Hotels.com, Hotwire, Book-it, Booking.com, etc. Wow, I know there are a lot of them. Once in a while I find a pricing anomaly where they are lower than Priceline Express Deal, and I know exactly which hotel I am going to get, that it is worth taking advantage of it. There is value sometimes in the certainty of which hotel you are getting and its location in the city you are going too.

If you have to go to certain hotel, always check the hotel's site for discounted rooms for AAA, AARP, Military/Government and weekend discounts. Sometimes these rates are better than the travel sites. Lastly, when you do finally book your room and arrive at the front desk always make a plea for a king bed and a complimentary upgrade. Are you a member of the hotels loyalty program? Well, let them know about this upon check in and get the same benefits as if you booked directly with the hotel.

Ask for a complementary bottle of water, they have it behind the desk. This works for me more often than not and it is the continuation of my stacking and bundling mentality. The same logic that I just explained goes for flights, rental cars, cruises and vacation packages. You need to do as much homework as possible and prepare a logical range for what the best price can be and go after it with everything you've got. The general rule is the more flexible and open to change that you are, the better discounts you will be able to get for your travel.

I always try to balance these two competing variables, savings versus convenience. Some things are worth paying a little extra for while other things are a total waste of money. Luckily the choice is always yours to make!

FREELOTTO

Although I am not a big fan of playing lotteries as part of my plan for building wealth, sometimes I get the itch when I am feeling lucky. That is when I go to Freelotto.com to try my luck. I have played the lottery off and on for years, and have never really hit anything big. I have won a $1 here, or $5 there, once in a while, and they have paid out by sending a check in the mail. I am not really sure what would happen if you did hit one of the big lotteries that they offer? I do know that I have used this site to play the lottery for 6 games a day for over a year and never won anything. This serves to remind me that playing the lottery is a huge waste of time and money. Thankfully I didn't spend any money to learn this lesson. Yes, they have a mobile app.

BUYING A CAR

Is it time to buy a new car? Are you ready to go to the dealership to test drive the latest model and negotiate your best deal? Whoa there, hold on a second. You will need to do ten times the research to be ready for a purchase of this size. Start with TrueCar and Kelly Blue Book apps for your phone. You will need TrueCar to look at the real price of the car, dealer invoice and what others have recently paid for the car you are interested in. You will need the Kelly Blue Book app for your trade in, if you have one, to make sure they are offering you a fair deal. When you negotiate just remember the longer it takes the better deal you will get.

Also, once you think you finally have your ideal price, start stacking and bundling. Do they offer a military discount, credit union, AMEX, AARP, AAA, or any other affiliation discount? Many times the answer is yes and you can stack up as many as you can justify. What else will they throw in or "bundle" with the deal? Free floor mats and mud flaps? A full tank of gas and another gift card for your next fill up? How about free lifetime inspections and/or oil changes. Make a list of what is most important to you ahead of time, when there is no pressure so you are ready to ask when the time is right. Can you pay for the final cash settlement that you owe with a credit card? If so, there is an additional 1% back in your pocket.

Also, when you are all done and have your best deal in hand and you are driving home, try to think of other things that you may have wanted or forgot to ask for. Write them down once you are home as you will be back to the dealership again for your first service.

I would go back in and ask for more. Remember they still need you. You are now a customer; you can refer people to the dealership with good word of mouth since everyone is going to ask you "hey, where did you get your new car"?

Typically, the dealership will pay you a referral fee for every customer that you send in that buys a car. This will wear off after about 6 months so take advantage of this opportunity as quickly as you can. Also, the dealership usually gets rated by the manufacturer of the vehicle. They send out a customer satisfaction surveys that links to their bonus opportunities. Until you fill out the survey they will do whatever they can to keep the buying experience a very positive one. Keep this in mind and use it to your advantage if you can.

BUYING A HOUSE

When it is time to buy a house you need to make sure you understand the market you are looking to buy into very well. You will want to load www.Zillow.com and www.Realtor.com apps to help give you a sense of the market in your area. Also, make sure whatever broker or agent you choose is also a participating member of Upromise.

You can pick up an additional 1/3% of the homes sale price, up to $3000, in cash back (see terms and conditions). You also have a huge opportunity to utilize all three strategies at one time in one transaction. You can stack discounts, and bundle in extras and link in new cash streams. That is why real estate transactions have made so many people rich once they discovered and mastered the tricks of the trade.

SECTION 2 – Sell side transactions (revenue generation)

In this section I will teach you about strategies that you can use to make money (revenue generation) by using mobile apps as an enabler to create the environment where you get paid.

LINKEDIN

This is another essential mobile application that I use every day to conduct business. It is the premier app for all my business connections, where I can network, share ideas, learn about new subjects, join groups and find new sources of revenues. Yes, you can actually make money on Linkedin if you know how. You need to make connections with people who can set you on the right course.

This may be in the form of finding the right mentor, supplier, expert consultant or your dream job. Sometimes recruiters are looking for freelancers to perform projects or to fill short term consulting jobs. You need to actually take the time to build out a professional looking profile and make thoughtful connections that add value to you and your network. Like most things in life you need to give to get something back. Help others as much as you can and the favor will be returned before you know it. Sometimes when you least expect it.

Many people have created opportunities that eventually turned into something good and profitable. They have received offers and invitations to special events, speaking engagements, mini-consulting opportunities, co-authoring a paper or eBook, paid research or surveys. This list can go on and on.

FACEBOOK AND TWITTER

Even though LinkedIn is my preferred site for "social networking" I cannot ignore the opportunities that both Facebook and Twitter often in terms of connecting with people and making some money. Like any other forum where you are connected with people and companies, there are opportunities to learn and share. You can also sell things to people and market your own products if you have any. Sometimes I see companies offering special promotions only to their Facebook groups.

It is certainly worth connecting with them and liking their site to get opportunities for saving on products and services you use. However, the real value is in your ability to sell things to "liked minded" and connected friends and family. A good example is a stay-at-home mother who is connected to 30 other stay-at-home mothers. If you want to get rid of a stroller, all you have to do is post one message and it will be sold within an hour. Now that is powerful online sales. These types of groups are sharing savings and earnings ideas, coupons (some are "extreme couponers"), startup ideas and eventually become entrepreneurs.

Twitter is another way to build a loyal following and have influence over a large group of people that might be receptive to your products and/or services. There is really no end to the number of ideas and opportunities that a connected group could bring to the savvy online marketer.

EBAY AND AMAZON

I know this may seem obvious but selling your things on EBay and Amazon is a great way to make extra money. The mobile apps make it easier than ever to quickly list an item and track your views, watchers and bids. I try to bundle a bunch of items together so it is easy to manage and track. EBay lets you list ten items per month without any listing fees. Go to your basement and/or attic with your Smartphone and start taking pictures until you hit ten items.

With the EBay app loaded on your smartphone anytime you get a bid on one of your items your phone alarms. It plays the sound of a cash register ringing and you get a little EBAY symbol in your notification bar at the top of your phone.

Since I sleep with my cell phone next to me on the night stand, it is awesome to be lying in bed and hear the cash register ringing as people place bids while I sleep. With your mobile phone and EBay you can literally make money in your sleep! If you run out of good items to sell on EBay because you are so good at it, turn those skills into a business by selling other peoples items for them for a commission. There are so many non-technical people out there that would have tremendous difficulty in listing and selling items. Well, do it for them and make some cash.

Do you want to take your skills and this process to the next level? Open an EBay/Amazon digital storefront. That's right, you need to contact product manufacturers and become a wholesaler or dealer for a line of new products. You want to sell the latest gadget or popular toys, now you can and do it profitably and run it all from the palm of your hand. You are only limited by your time and imagination when it comes to ideas for online businesses.

EBOOK

Have you ever considering writing? Do you have any expertise or an interesting story to tell? Amazon KDP (Kindle Direct Publishing) has made it easier than ever to publish your own eBook and get it listed for sale. All you have to do it put some ideas together, write up an outline, do some research, and write up the content. You could have this all pulled together in a couple of weeks and published within a few days once you have your account setup and everything ready to go.

If you do a good job and attract some attention in the Kindle bookstore the royalties will come rolling in. At the 70% royalty level this can add up to some real money coming in every month. Think about it, write the book once and collect the money forever as long as the book continues to sell. If you can crank out a new title every month or so is like creating a new business and putting it on auto-pilot. The perfect turn-key business!

If you dread the idea of being hunched over a computer all day long pecking away at the keyboard in frustration, worry no longer. Your Smartphone will come to the rescue! Just buy a good quality Bluetooth wireless headset with good noise cancelation. Pair that up with Google Docs on your Smartphone and let it do all the work for you. Dictate using speech-to-text voice recognition wherever and whenever you like. Most of this book was dictated using this technique.

I like to go for long walks which get my mind turning with ideas, so I pull out my phone and start dictating those ideas.

I can then clean things up and get them in the proper format later when I get home.

ONLINE SURVEYS

The Internet is flush with online survey sites that offer opportunities to make some quick extra cash or gift cards. Like all other sites on the Internet, there are good sites and there are bad sites. The trick to finding the best sites is by using good common sense by doing a little research on the offerings. I usually poke around the site to see how it looks, how professional it seems, the types of surveys they offer, and how they payout. You can find the payment information on the sites FAQ (frequently asked questions) page or in their terms and conditions at the bottom of the main page.

There are generally two types of survey companies for you to think about. The first type offers generic consumer feedback that anyone with the time and patience can complete. They are usually very frequent, short in duration and low paying. I grow tired of this type very quickly and tend to get bored with them. However, money is money! If you have the spare time, these surveys can add up quickly like anything else. How many $5 ten minutes survey can you do per week about consumer products?

I tend to stay away from companies that offer "points" instead of cash for doing the work. There are usually minimum point thresholds that you have to meet before you can cash out. I always seem to get close to the threshold and then the offers seem to dry up, and I am left waiting and anticipating the next survey offer. When the next offer finally does come and I am able to qualify and complete the survey, I usually cash out and delete the bookmark to their site from my web browser.

The second type of company focuses more on niche industries such as education, science, technology or healthcare. These types of surveys come less often, are longer (20 to 30 minutes) and pay significantly more money, $50 to $200 per survey. These are better for most people if you have the expertise in an area of demand. Just do a Google search for your specialty and add the keywords "paid survey", a good potential list will come up for your review. (I. E. Teacher paid surveys)

You will have to fill out an online profile to prove that you fit the niche community and in many cases join an online panel of experts. It should only take a few minutes to complete the questionnaire and boom, you're in. A couple times per week you will get an e-mail from them telling you about a new survey opportunity for your consideration. You click on the link on your phone and complete a quick screener to make sure you have the expertise and fit the survey demographic requirements and then you're in.

Twenty minutes later or so and you have a check for $50 to $75 on its way to you in the mail or through PayPal. Depending upon the size and demand of the niche your expertise is in, there may be dozens of companies that are doing research in your particular field of study. If you can track them all down and join all their research panels, you could be getting two to three e-mails per days or more. How does an extra $200 to $300 dollars per day in cash sound to you? It is possible for the right person that has the right expertise and the time to complete surveys on their phone.

How about a stay-at-home mother that quit her corporate job to raise her children? This might be a perfect fit that allows her the freedom and flexibility, which raising children demands, while putting all her expertise to good use. She would also be contributing to the family income and/or maybe for herself for a much needed spa day. The real beauty in doing online surveys is that you really are your own boss. If a survey comes in and you are too busy or not feeling up to it, you can save it for later or hit delete!

Once you get listed on some of these research panels, others panels looking to recruit new members will reach out to you, or your name is sold to them, either way you will get invitations to join new panels. The more panels and research groups you join the more invitations you will get from others. It is like the NESTING effect where it becomes a self sustaining system.

I do think that there is a finite limit as to the number of panels one human being can handle, so it helps to know your limits. It would also be wise to really spruce up your online profiles and social networking presence so that recruiters can see that you are an expert in your field. Your LinkedIn profile should be the focus of these efforts and should show this very clearly. This is a clear example of the LINKING strategy at work; you put a ton of effort into your LinkedIn profile showing your expertise, which attracts others to want to link into you.

The people in your network will help validate you as an expert which will bring all kinds of revenue generating opportunities to you. Do not underestimate the power of your online profile and presence. Please take the time to make sure everything is done at the professional level showcasing you and your skills to the world. If you do this correctly, the world will notice and respond in kind.

There are companies searching the LinkedIn database looking for experts to do "micro-consulting" jobs. These are small consulting jobs that can be done from anywhere (with the Internet and a Smartphone) within a few hours or a few days at a very attractive rate. Some may have called this "freelance" work but the more modern term is micro-consulting. This is a focused group with a niche where the people that are the best positioned to tap into this lucrative revenue source will reap huge rewards.

Think about it for a minute, someone from LinkedIn requests to connect to you that you don't know. You are a nice and trusting person so you agree. Five minutes after accepting their offer to connect you receive an e-mail stating they have reviewed your profile and they are very impressed with your accomplishments. Further, they have an opportunity for someone with your skill set to consider. It's an offer to complete 4 hours of research for a particular subject that you are an expert in. Going rate is $250 per hour and the work needs completed by the end of the week.

You accept the project and are paid $1000 flat fee for your efforts which may have taken only two hours since you are an expert in this area and are very motivated to earn such a premium rate. Sometimes this work may require some online research or networking with your peers. Other times you may need to take some phone calls to answer questions regarding a study or project they need your advice on. Either way you are doing it from the comfort of your LazyBoy using your Smartphone.

BLOGGING

If you can find a niche in the blogging world and you can create a nice following, you can turn this into a steady income stream. This is accomplished by adding some advertising banner bars or side bars to your blog. You will get paid on a per click basis for all the ads that are listed on your site. They are typically rotated and refreshed by the ad company.

The most popular one is Adwords by Google. But there are many others out there as well. Like anything else, you will need to do your homework and find the right advertising partners that fit your site and profit goals.

The other trick used by bloggers is capturing e-mail addresses of people that visit their blog. These addresses are valuable as they can be used to send out offers for products and services related to the blog topic. They can also be sold to other companies that sell into the same category. Although this is a way to make additional profits, you need to balance this with the loyalty that you have to your blog, and the people that put their faith into you when they submit their e-mail addresses.

If you think blogging might be for you, please check out Google (https://support.google.com/blogger/answer/1623800?hl=en) BlogSpot as a good starting place and a free resource to get you going. The other good site to check out and consider is www.Wordpress.com where you can setup and manage your own blog or website for free for the basic version. This should be enough to get you started until you are ready for an upgrade.

AFFILIATE MARKETING

Affiliate marketing is the simple idea of getting paid by directing traffic from your website to another that leads to a site registration and/or sale. The more traffic you send to a site the more money you make. Further, the more traffic you send that actually buys a product the more money you make. So let's say that I set up my own blog about personal finance and I signed up for a Google Adwords account. I will get paid simply by allowing Google to post these rotating ads on my site. That is a good start and a revenue source, however what if I become an affiliate for a personal finance magazine and purposefully promote a link to their site on my blog.

For every person that clicks that link, 1) I get paid a fee per click and 2) if the person subscribes to that magazine I get paid $15. If you are able to build a significant following on your blog this strategy can become a meaningful revenue source. The main thing to remember with blogging is that you are offering your audience a free service. You need to focus on and make sure you are offering a value to them, and that you are truly helping people. Just putting a bunch of information about a subject on a blog is not going to gain you a following. You need to get involved and build trust and relationships that last.

If you can do that, the blog will grow quickly through word of mouth and social media. With that said, it doesn't hurt to use some good old marketing and self promotion.

Don't be afraid to write articles for other people's blogs, magazines and websites. Do some free public speaking or be on an expert panel for a local association or group. Help answer questions in online forums and be useful to others in their business. This will bring attention to you and your blog. It's OK to tell people about your blog on LinkedIn, Facebook, Twitter, Google +, Hangouts, and other sites you can find. You have to put yourself out there for things to come your way. If you do write an eBook, make reference to your blog in the book. Find a way to LINK everything you do to everything else you are doing.

YOUTUBE

Have you ever done something crazy and recorded it with
your Smartphone? Are you musically talented or a hilarious
comedian? If you are, then maybe you could create a
YouTube video that could go "viral" on the Internet.
Perhaps you are an excellent teacher and can take complex
subjects and make them simple. Whatever angle you can
dream up and get yourself noticed on the Internet might
become a new income stream for you. Once you have a
substantial amount of views for your YouTube video,
Google will allow you to enable ADwords which will
stream rotation advertising before or during your video.
You will get commissions for every view of that
advertisement. This can grow into a nice income for
someone with a viral video.

Some people have put together a series of short videos on
how to do this, or how to fix that. How to plays songs on
the piano or the guitar, whatever you know how to do. You
need to take a self assessment and take credit for your
skills, and then think about how you can commercialize and
monetize those assets. Practical videos can do OK, but the
crazy and hilarious videos seem to get the most views.
Think of Americans Funniest Videos!

VIRTUAL ASSISTANTS

Virtual Assistants (VA) are people that do "information" based work for other people for an hourly fee. Busy executives or entrepreneurs don't have time to read all those e-mails and respond to them. Think about someone who has made it to the top of their field. They are overwhelmed with requests for speaking engagements, meetings, calls, mail, e-mails, memo's, scheduling, paying bills and the myriad of personal responsibilities as well. They are more than happy to pay someone to take on the responsibilities for taking care of all of these items for them.

Competitive market rates are $25 to $30 per hour for this type of work. And with the Smartphone and the Internet the VA can literally be anywhere doing this work for them. Are you trustworthy and reliable? Are you a good communicator and an aggressive listener? Do you have good technology and research skills? Maybe this is the job for you? Well, where do I apply for such a job? You start your own business!

You advertise your services targeting companies with executives and entrepreneurs. You look for agencies that "handle" celebrities and busy rich people.

All you need to do is find that one person that is willing to give you a chance, even part-time to prove yourself. If you do an excellent job for them, the word will spread quickly until you have two or three customers. Chances are good that they will keep you busy enough that you will not need any more to keep you occupied full-time. Who knows maybe you will become successful enough that you will need your own virtual assistant!

INTERNATIONAL

If you haven't noticed it yet, the world is getting flatter and smaller. The Internet is expanding globally and people all around the world are learning how to use it to make money. China and India are exploding with business and tech savvy entrepreneurs. This expansion is leveling the playing field for anyone who has a Smartphone, the Internet, and some ambition. There is a huge opportunity for people all over the world to compete for your business. You need to join the game and get your piece of the pie. Think of it, you now have the entire connected world as your opportunity to sell your products and services as well.

I am focusing my international efforts on India right now as I have been making some very good connections with some professional, smart and ambitious people on LinkedIn. This has presented me with new opportunities to do business in their country. It is very exciting to be working internationally from my home on my Smartphone serving customers in India. You really need to open your eyes to the global market and see how you can help others. I am also willing to volunteer my expertise when I can to make new connections and learn about other countries and cultures.

If you can imagine the global opportunities that you have right now, it is actually quite amazing and overwhelming. You literally have the entire connected world at your fingertips. The real question is what are you going to do about it? What steps are you going to take to be noticed and to connect with those around the planet? I think the best approach is going to be an incremental one. Take those baby steps to get things started and then let the momentum build as you develop expertise and automate the process. Don't forget to hire a virtual assistant as things grow out of your individual control.

Think about what you can do with all the tools sets that we have discussed so far in this book. Connect with people using Facebook, Twitter, Google +, LinkedIn and any other tools set you can find. Make connections with people that you share something in common. Share ideas with them and most importantly learn about their country, their cultures and their problems. Help them if you can and look for creative ways to solve their problems.

Chances are good that if you can solve a problem for one person that there are millions more out there with the same problem that you just solved. Now you have the opportunity to use what you know and create an app or automation to solve it for the masses.

Don't forget that helping people is the key to developing a winning strategy. If you know someone does not have the ability to pay for a service, do not try to charge them. The good karma and the relationships that you build will come back to you tenfold. Stay positive and always ask what more can I do for you. If you can follow this philosophy you will find that others will do anything they can to help you as well.

AUTOMATION

A lot has been written these days about automating your life so that you are more efficient and more disciplined about doing the right thing to stay on track with your budget and investments. I have to say that I use this thinking as much as I can for efficiency and for time savings more than for budgeting or investing discipline. I really like the mobile banking application offered by my bank. I regularly get checks in the mail but rarely have the time to run to the bank to cash them.

Using my Smartphone to scan and deposit the check it a huge time saver. Same goes for online bill pay, it is really easy to setup recurring payments of my bills so I no longer have to worry about them anymore.

With that said, I still check them very closely every month to make sure they correct. Try to automate as much as you can to make your life easier and more efficient. Can you automate other things in your life that will save you time or money? Can you automate small processes that make you money with little or no effort? You need to shape your thinking about maximizing your time for everything you are working on. If I can save 5 minutes per task but I do that task 10 times per day it is a huge savings for me and well worth the automation process.

CONCLUSION

There are so many Smartphone applications that are emerging each and every day that is it hard to discuss and describe them all. I tried to stay away from listing each and every website and mobile app that I use,

and tried to take the time to explain the logic in how I use the applications or website. You can Google search for sites/apps and you will find a long list for each and every category that I described. You can select the app that fits your mobile OS and your preference. It is how you use the app that I am mostly concerned about, and the strategies that you build around its capabilities that matter most.

Please study and think about the strategies that I introduced to you throughout this book. The ideas of STACKING your discounts, BUNDLING your purchases to get more value, NESTING and LINKING your investments and your online profile into a new electronic ecosystem, and lastly can you combine more than one of them together?

There is no limit to what you can do with strategies. Play with them, improve them, create new ones, and be creative and imaginative.

I can tell you that the key to getting these items in place is to get moving now. Don't wait and don't delay. If you can do even one item and get it done within the next 24 hours you will feel good about yourself. You need to push yourself and set hard to reach goals and make yourself do it. Wealth does not build itself; you need to make it happen every day. Once you get an item completed you can start to build momentum by quickly doing another item. Build this thinking into everything you do and make it part of your DNA.

CONNECT WITH ME!

I am very interested in connecting with you. I want to expand my network of "like minded" professionals with whom I can share my thoughts, ideas and strategies. Please click on the link below and connect with me on LinkedIn. Let me know that you read this book so that I may honor your request to connect.

http://www.linkedin.com/pub/thomas-johnson/11/a84/bbb/

Also, I have started a blog to continue to share updates on new apps that I have found, as well as, the strategies that get the most out of them to make and save you money. Check out: www.smartmoneytech.com

Lastly, and most importantly to me, the author, if you found the information in this book to be of any value to you, please rate it positively. It is VERY important for an author to get good ratings for their books to get them listed and noticed by others. I hope you will support my efforts.

Thanks for taking the time to read this book. I look forward to connecting with you and continuing the conversation.

My Best,

Thomas H. Johnson

www.ingramcontent.com/pod-product-compliance
Lightning Source LLC
Chambersburg PA
CBHW071009180526
45168CB00003B/1354